C000092215

HEALTHY RECIPES FOR BEGINNERS

APPETIZERS

Paola Clifford

Welcome!

To this new series of book, inspired by all the recipes I know thanks to my great passion: *cooking!*

"You really know what you are eating if you make it yourself"

In this book you will find many different ideas for your dishes, with ingredients from all around the world, with a Gourmet touch!

Thanks to these cookbooks you can develop your cooking skills for any kind of meal, as you'll find recipes for:

- ★ salads
- ★ sides
- ★ lunch
- ★ dinner
- ★ Desserts

And much more...

Whether your favourite dish is French fries, muffins, chicken tenders or grilled vegetables, with this series of books you will learn how to do it with a better-looking touch!

Don't forget that this books have also low fat recipes with healthy ingredients to *keep you fit and have a healthier meal plan!*

Remember that having a wide variety of ingredients and foods in your diet have many benefits for you, that's why you will find ingredients from:

- ★ Asia
- ★ Russia
- ★ America
- ★ Europe

And much more...

Since I started to pay more attention on the decision of the ingredients and how to plate a dish, I enjoy cooking a lot more! That's why I made this cookbook for all of you that want to develop your cooking skills and start eating healthier!

I hope you will enjoy this book! Don't forget to check out the other ones from the collection, and enjoy your time in the kitchen!

HEALTHY RECIPES
FOR BEGINNERS

APPETIZERS

LEARN HOW TO MIX DIFFERENT INGREDIENTS AND SPICES TO
CREATE DELICIOUS DISHES AND BUILD A COMPLETE MEAL PLAN!
THI COOKBOOK INCLUDES QUICK AND EASY RECIPES TO
PREPARE ON A DAILY BASIS, FOR AN EFFECTIVE DIET AND A HEAL-
THIER LIFESTYLE!

Paola Clifford

HEALTHY RECIPES FOR BEGINNERS: APPETIZERS

Learn how to mix different ingredients and spices to create delicious dishes and build a complete meal plan! This cookbook includes quick recipes to prepare on a daily basis, for an effective diet and a healthier lifestyle!

HEALTHY RECIPES FOR BEGINNERS: SIDES

Learn how to mix different ingredients and spices to create delicious dishes and build a complete meal plan! This cookbook includes quick recipes to prepare on a daily basis, for an effective diet and a healthier lifestyle!

HEALTHY RECIPES FOR BEGINNERS: QUICK AND EASY

Learn how to mix different ingredients and spices to create delicious dishes and build a complete meal plan! This cookbook includes quick-and-easy recipes to prepare on a daily basis, for an effective diet and a Healthier lifestyle for your 2021!

HEALTHY RECIPES FOR BEGINNERS: LUNCH

Learn how to mix different ingredients and spices to create delicious dishes and build a complete meal plan! This cookbook includes quick recipes to prepare on a daily basis, for an effective diet and a healthier lifestyle!

HEALTHY RECIPES FOR BEGINNERS: DESSERTS

Learn how to mix different ingredients and fruit to create delicious desserts and build a complete meal plan! This cookbook includes quick and easy recipes for both adults and kids, from the Mediterranean and other well-known diets!

HEALTHY RECIPES FOR BEGINNERS: TOP 50

Learn how to mix different ingredients to create Delicious meals and build a complete meal plan for your diet! This cookbook includes quick-and-easy recipes for all your family. Amaze your friends with your cooking skills!

HEALTHY RECIPES FOR BEGINNERS: SALADS

Lose weight by eating well! Learn how to mix different ingredients and fruit to create delicious salads and build a complete meal plan! This cookbook includes quick and easy recipes for both adults and kids, from the mediterranean and other well-known diets!

HEALTHY RECIPES FOR BEGINNERS: DINNER

Learn how to mix different ingredients and spices to create delicious dishes and build a complete meal plan! This cookbook includes quick and easy recipes to prepare on a daily basis, for an effective diet and a healthier lifestyle!

SALADS AND LUNCH MEAL PREP

2 books in 1: Healthy salad and lunch recipes for beginners. Lose weight by eating well! This cookbook contains some of the best low-fat recipes that also ideal for weight loss and body-healing routines. Improve your cooking skills with the right book!

COMPLETE DINNER COOKBOOK

This boundle contains 3 recipe books in 1: healthy dinner, desserts and sides recipes for beginner.

Learn how to use different ingredients, herbs, spices and plants to cook delicious dishes for your complete meal plan.

Table of Contents

Sommario

SOME YUMMY BITES FOR ANY OCCASION

Drunken Stuffed Figs

Serving: 12

Ingredients

- 24 fresh figs

- 1 cup cognac

- 1 cup mascarpone cheese

- 1/2 cup confectioners' sugar

- 1 1/2 cups toasted hazelnuts

- 2 tablespoons chopped fresh mint leaves

Direction

- Inject figs with 1 tbsp. cognac with a marinade injector baste, evenly dividing amount among figs. Chill in fridge while prepping the other ingredients.

- Blend 3/4 confectioners' sugar, mascarpone cheese and leftover cognac in medium bowl; chill in fridge while prepping other ingredients.

- In food processor/blender, mix leftover confectioners' sugar, mint leaves and toasted hazelnuts; put mixture in medium bowl.

- Remove fig stems. Lengthwise, cut in half. Use even portions of mascarpone cheese mixture and cognac to fill halves. Roll in hazelnut mixture. Put, cheese side up, on medium serving platter. Chill till serving in the fridge.

Nutrition Information

- Calories: 335 calories;
- Total Carbohydrate: 27.2
- Cholesterol: 23
- Protein: 4.6
- Total Fat: 19.2

Easy Bruschetta

Serving: 16

Ingredients

- 1 French baguette, cut into 1/2 inch thick circles

- 8 plum tomatoes, diced

- 1 cup chopped fresh basil

- 1/2 red onion, minced

- freshly ground black pepper

- 3 cloves garlic

Direction

- Heat the oven to 200°C or 400°F.

- In one small mixing bowl, mix basil, red onion and tomato; combine thoroughly. Add freshly ground black pepper to season. Put aside.

- On baking sheet, place the bread. Put inside the oven, and bake for about 5 minutes, till nicely toasted.

- Take bread out of oven, and turn on one big serving platter. Cool bread for 3 to 5 minutes. Rub top of every toast slice with garlic; toast must glisten with garlic. Scoop mixture of tomato liberally on every slice to serve.

Nutrition Information

- Calories: 90 calories;

- Sodium: 186

- Total Carbohydrate: 17.8

- Cholesterol: 0

- Protein: 3.8

- Total Fat: 0.6

Easy Butternut Squash Ravioli

Serving: 6

Ingredients

- 1 cup mashed, cooked butternut squash

- 1/2 teaspoon salt

- 1/2 teaspoon freshly ground black pepper

- 1 pinch cayenne pepper

- 1/2 cup mascarpone cheese

- 1 egg yolk

- 1/3 cup grated Parmesan cheese

- 1 (16 ounce) package round wonton wrappers

- 2 tablespoons butter

- 1 clove garlic, unpeeled

- chopped fresh sage to taste

- 1 tablespoon grated Parmesan cheese, or to taste

Direction

- Into a mixing bowl, put cooked squash. Put in cayenne pepper, black pepper and salt. Mix in 1/3 cup Parmesan cheese, egg yolk and mascarpone cheese, whisking till the filling is smoothly incorporated.

- Onto a working surface, put a wonton wrapper. In water, wet the tip of a finger, and run it all around the outer edge of the wonton skin to moisten. Put a teaspoon of filling in the middle of the wonton. Fold the wonton in half to create a half-moon form, and pinch the edges to secure. Redo with the rest of wonton wrappers.

- Set a deep skillet over medium-low heat. Mix in butter and unpeeled clove of garlic. In the meantime, boil a saucepan of lightly salted water.

- Into the boiling water, drop the filled raviolis, a few at a time, and cook for 2 minutes till they float to the top. Allow the raviolis to drain, and put into the skillet. Turn the heat underneath the skillet to medium-high, and cook for 2 or 3 more minutes just till the raviolis are infused with garlic flavor. Scatter over more Parmesan cheese, additional black pepper and chopped sage to taste.

Nutrition Information

- Calories: 378 calories;
- Total Fat: 15.9
- Sodium: 742
- Total Carbohydrate: 47.4
- Cholesterol: 79
- Protein: 11.5

Easy Chicken Liver Pate

Serving: 16

Ingredients

- 1 cup butter, divided
- 1 onion, quartered
- 1 tart apple - peeled, cored, and quartered
- 1 pound chicken livers, rinsed and trimmed
- 1/4 cup brandy
- 2 tablespoons heavy whipping cream
- 1 teaspoon lemon juice
- 1 1/2 teaspoons salt
- 1/4 teaspoon ground black pepper
- 1 tablespoon butter, melted

Direction

- Let 1/2 cup of butter soften by setting it aside.

- Put in the apple and onion in steel knife blade food processor; then coarsely chop by turning the processor on.

- Place a large skillet on the stove and turn on to medium heat and put in 3 tablespoons butter into the skillet to melt. Add in the apple and onion; cook and mix for 5 to 10 minutes until it becomes lightly brown. Then put back the apple and onion to the food processor.

- Using the same skillet but on high heat, put in 5 tablespoons butter to melt. Minimize the heat and add in the brandy; without stirring, let it heat. Gently light the liquid using a lighter or a match; then let the flame calm down.

- Place the chicken liver mixture to the food processor together with apple and onion. Add in the cream and mix until the texture becomes smooth. Then put the mixture into a bowl and place inside the refrigerator for at least 30 minutes until chilled.

- Get the softened 1/2 cup of butter that you set aside into pieces and then put in the food processor; mix in about 1/3 of the liver mixture then blend for 5 seconds. Do it again for 2 more times with left liver mixture. Add in the pepper, salt, and lemon juice then mix well.

- Place the pate in small dishes or in a serving dish; put 1 tablespoon of melted butter on top of it. Use a plastic wrap to cover; then place inside the refrigerator for about 3 hours until chilled.

Nutrition Information

- Calories: 165 calories;
- Total Fat: 14.1

- Sodium: 320

- Total Carbohydrate: 2.7

- Cholesterol: 137

Easy Salmon Pate

Serving: 6

Ingredients

- 3 1/2 cups smoked salmon, torn or cut into bite-sized pieces

- 6 (7 ounce) containers creme fraiche

- 3 tablespoons freshly squeezed lemon juice, or more to taste

- freshly ground black pepper to taste

- 2 sprigs fennel fronds

Direction

- Mix together the lemon juice, a crushed coarse of black pepper, smoked salmon and crème

31

fraiche in a blender; Mix until the texture becomes smooth.

- Transfer into a bowl then modify seasoning, and let it chill for 1 hour until serving time. Add fennel fronds for garnish.

Nutrition Information

- Calories: 804 calories;
- Total Fat: 81.4
- Sodium: 694
- Total Carbohydrate: 7.9
- Cholesterol: 302
- Protein: 21.7

Eggplant Caponata (Sicilian Version)

Serving: 16

Ingredients

- 2 tablespoons red wine vinegar
- 2 teaspoons white sugar
- 1 teaspoon salt
- ground black pepper to taste
- 2 teaspoons minced fresh parsley, or to taste
- salt to taste
- 1/4 cup olive oil, divided
- 1 cup finely chopped celery
- 1 onion, finely chopped
- 1 clove garlic, minced
- 1 eggplant, peeled and cut into 1/2-inch cubes

- 1 1/2 cups canned plum tomatoes, drained and coarsely chopped

- 12 green olives, pitted and coarsely chopped

- 1 1/2 tablespoons drained capers

- 1 tablespoon tomato paste

- 1 teaspoon minced oregano

Direction

- Sprinkle eggplant with salt then put in a colander set over a bowl. Let it stand for about 30 minutes then rinse and pat dry eggplant.

- In a big pan set over medium temperature, heat 2 tablespoons olive oil. Add celery and cook for about 4 minutes or until tender. Stir often as it cooks. Toss in onion and garlic. Continue to cook and stir for about 5 minutes until onion is tender and lightly golden. Use a slotted spoon to scoop the mixture and transfer to a bowl.

- In the same pan, heat 2 tablespoons olive oil that remains. Toss in eggplant and cook for 5-7 minutes or until lightly browned. Stir constantly as it cooks. Mix in tomatoes, capers, tomato paste, olives, oregano and the celery mixture. Cook to a boil then turn down heat to low. Remove cover and let it simmer for about 15 minutes until caponata is thickened.

- Season with salt, pepper, sugar and vinegar to taste. Serve in a bowl garnished with parsley.

Nutrition Information

- Calories: 56 calories;

- Cholesterol: 0

- Protein: 0.9

- Total Fat: 3.9

- Sodium: 297

- Total Carbohydrate: 5.5

Escargot Mushrooms

Serving: 6

Ingredients

- 4 tablespoons butter

- 2 cloves garlic, minced

- 6 helix snails, without shells

- 6 large fresh mushrooms

Direction

- Heat garlic and butter in a medium pot on medium heat. Put the snails in the pot and cook for 5 minutes until tender.

- Get rid of the mushroom stems. Scoop a half teaspoon of melted butter and garlic in the mushroom caps. Microwave the mushrooms for 2-3 minutes. Place the snails inside the mushroom caps and microwave for another 3min.

Nutrition Information

- Calories: 88 calories;

- Total Carbohydrate: 1.9

- Cholesterol: 27

- Protein: 3.2

- Total Fat: 7.8

- Sodium: 73

Escargots Vol Au Vent

Serving: 4

Ingredients

- 1 tablespoon finely minced fresh parsley
- 1 teaspoon freshly ground black pepper
- 1/8 teaspoon ground nutmeg
- 2 tablespoons dry white wine
- 12 puff pastry shells
- 12 helix snails, without shells
- 1/2 cup butter, softened
- 2 cloves garlic, finely chopped
- 1 green onion, finely chopped
- 12 mushroom caps

Direction

- Preheat the oven to 400°F (200°C). Drain the escargots and rinse it off in cold water then drain it again.

- Mix the green onion, pepper, butter, wine, garlic, parsley and nutmeg together in a mixing bowl. Mix well. Fill every pastry shell with 1 teaspoon of the butter mixture. Put a layer of 1 escargot, another teaspoon of the butter mixture and a mushroom cap on top.

- Put the filled pastry shells on a 15x10-inch baking sheet. Put in preheated oven and bake for 8-10 minutes until it turns golden brown in color.

Nutrition Information

- Calories: 838 calories;

- Sodium: 911

- Total Carbohydrate: 53.5

- Cholesterol: 81

- Protein: 21.3

Fig And Olive Tapenade

Serving: 6 | Prep: 15mins | Cook: 10mins | Ready in:

Ingredients

- 1/3 cup chopped toasted walnuts

- 1 (8 ounce) package cream cheese

- 1 teaspoon dried thyme

- 1/4 teaspoon cayenne pepper

- 2/3 cup chopped kalamata olives

- 2 cloves garlic, minced

- salt and pepper to taste

- 1 cup chopped dried figs

- 1/2 cup water

- 1 tablespoon olive oil

- 2 tablespoons balsamic vinegar

1 teaspoon dried rosemary

Direction

- In a saucepan placed on medium heat, put in the water and figs. Allow it to boil and let the figs cook until the liquid reduces, and the figs have softened. Remove the pan from heat and mix in the balsamic vinegar, thyme, olive oil, cayenne and rosemary. Mix in the garlic and olives thoroughly. Put pepper and salt to taste. Cover the pan and keep in the fridge for 4 hours or throughout the night for the flavors to combine.

- Remove the packaging wrapper from the block of cream cheese then put it on a serving platter. Put the tapenade mixture on top of the cream cheese and finish off with a sprinkle of walnuts

on top. Serve with crackers or sliced French
bread on the side.

Nutrition Information

- Calories: 327 calories;

- Sodium: 361

- Total Carbohydrate: 26.4

- Cholesterol: 41

- Protein: 5.2

- Total Fat: 24

Figs Oozing With Goat Cheese

Serving: 4

Ingredients

- 8 fresh figs

- 1/2 cup goat cheese, softened

- 8 grape leaves, drained and rinsed

- 1/2 cup honey

- skewers

Direction

- Preheat the grill to medium heat.
- At the bottom of every fig create a small incision big enough to hold a pastry bag tip. Put goat cheese into a pastry bag with a plain tip. Fill goat cheese into figs by squeezing a bit of cheese into every fig's bottom. The figs plump up when you fill them.

Wrap a grape leaf on every fig. On each skewer, skewer 2-3 figs.

- Oil the grate lightly. Put fig skewers onto hot grill. Cook, turning once for 2-3 minutes. Drizzle honey on. Serve.

Nutrition Information

- Calories: 272 calories;

- Total Fat: 5.7

- Sodium: 321

- Total Carbohydrate: 55.5

- Cholesterol: 14

- Protein: 5

Filipino Lumpia

Serving: 6

Ingredients

- 1 lumpia wrappers
- 1 pound ground beef
- 1/2 pound ground pork
- 1/3 cup finely chopped onion
- 1/3 cup finely chopped green bell pepper
- 1/3 cup finely chopped carrot
- 1 quart oil for frying

Direction

- Be sure that the lumpia wrappers are fully thawed. On a clean dry surface, lay several lumpia wrappers and use a damp towel to cover. The edges will dry out fast and wrappers are super thin.

- Mix carrot, green pepper, onion, ground pork, and beef in a medium bowl. Put about 2 tablespoons of the meat mixture along the middle of the wrapper. The filling should no larger around than your thumb or the wrapper will burn prior the meat is done. Then fold one edge of the wrapper over to the other. Turn the outer edges in slightly, and keep on rolling into a cylinder. Damp your finger, and wet the edge to enclose. Continue with the rest of the wrappers and filling, leaving completed lumpias covered to avoid drying. This is a nice time to ask a loved one or a friend to make the job less repetitive!
- In a 9-inch skillet set at medium to medium-high heat, add oil and heat to 365-375°F (170-175°C). Then fry 3 to 4 lumpia at a time. It should only take approximately 2 to 3 minutes for each side. It will be browned nicely once done. Transfer to paper towels to drain on.
- You can slice every lumpia into thirds for parties if you want. We pair the lumpia with banana ketchup in the Philippines, yet I've never seen it promoted in America.

Nutrition Information

- Calories: 365 calories;
- Total Fat: 30.2
- Sodium: 60
- Total Carbohydrate: 2.3
- Cholesterol: 75
- Protein: 20.4

Fried Morel Mushrooms

Serving: 4

Ingredients

- 1 pound morel mushrooms
- 1/2 cup oil for frying
- 2 eggs
- 3/4 cup milk
- 1 (4 ounce) packet saltine crackers, finely crushed
- salt and black pepper to taste

Direction

- Use a damp paper towel or a soft mushroom brush to clean the mushrooms. Cut any large mushrooms into half.
- Place the large skillet over medium heat and heat the oil. In a shallow bowl, whisk the eggs with milk. Dip the mushrooms into the egg and milk mixture to coat. Put the coated mushrooms into the cracker

crumbs and toss them well. Cook the coated mushrooms into the heated oil until their bottoms are golden brown. Take note that mushrooms cook quickly. Flip them over and cook the other side until browned.

- Place the browned mushrooms into the paper towel and allow them to drain. Sprinkle salt and pepper to taste.

Nutrition Information

- Calories: 255 calories;
- Sodium: 515
- Total Carbohydrate: 31.8
- Cholesterol: 97
- Protein: 10.5
- Total Fat: 10

Fried Peach And Pancetta Pizza

Serving: 4

Ingredients

- 8 ounces pancetta bacon, thickly sliced
- 1 teaspoon olive oil, or as needed
- 12 ounces pizza dough, or more to taste, cut into quarters
- 1 tablespoon all-purpose flour, or as needed
- 1 cup olive oil, or as needed
- 1/2 cup ricotta cheese
- 2 teaspoons chopped fresh thyme, or to taste
- ground black pepper to taste
- 20 slices fresh peach
- 1/4 cup freshly grated Parmigiano-Reggiano cheese, or to taste
- 4 teaspoons extra-virgin olive oil, or to taste

Direction

- Set oven to 245°C (475°F) to preheat. Use aluminum foil to line cookie sheets.

- Spread pancetta in a cold pan and pour a teaspoon of olive oil on pancetta. Stir and cook pancetta on medium heat for 5-10 minutes until it becomes brown and caramelized. Take off heat and let pancetta cool in oil in pan.

- Lightly dust a dough quarter with flour on a work surface; shape into an irregularly shaped crush of 1/8 inch thickness. Use your hands to mold dough so it has an even thickness; allow to rest 5 minutes on work surface. Repeat with the dough left.

- In a heavy cast iron pan on medium-high heat, heat a cup of olive oil it should reach a depth of 1/2 inch. Fry each dough piece for 2 minutes a side until it becomes brown and thoroughly cooked. The second side should be darker than the first. Transfer the crusts to paper towels and drain.

- Place pizza crusts, with the lighter side facing up on the prepared cookie sheets. Use the back of a spoon to spread 2 tablespoons of ricotta cheese on every crust. Add 1/2 teaspoon of fresh thyme on ricotta layer. Sprinkle the ricotta-thyme layer with pancetta; add black pepper to season. Place 5 slices of peach on every pizza, placing them around pancetta pieces. Spread a tablespoon of Parmesan-Reggiano cheese on every pizza. Pour a teaspoon of extra-virgin olive oil on top of Parmesan-Reggiano layer.

- Let it bake in the oven for 12-15 minutes, until cheese melts and peaches are soft and light brown. Leave on the cookie sheet to cool for 5-10 minutes.

Nutrition Information

- Calories: 504 calories;

- Total Fat: 25.8

- Sodium: 1098

- Total Carbohydrate: 46.3

- Cholesterol: 34

- Protein: 19.8

Fried Stuffed Squash Blossoms

Serving: 12

Ingredients

- 12 fresh zucchini blossoms

- 3/4 cup soft goat cheese at room temperature

- 1 egg yolk

- 1/4 cup shredded Gruyere cheese

- 1 pinch freshly ground black pepper, or to taste

- 1 pinch cayenne pepper

- Batter:

- 1 cup self-rising flour

- 1/2 cup cornstarch

- 1/4 cup ice-cold water, or as needed

- vegetable oil for frying

- 1 teaspoon all-purpose flour, or as needed

Direction

- Place lightly salted water in a pot and make it boil. Ready a large bowl of ice-cold water. Into the boiling water, place squash blossoms until wilted slightly, 30-45 seconds; put right away in the cold water to chill. Put to paper towels to strain.

- In a bowl, combine the cayenne pepper, black pepper, Gruyere cheese, egg yolk and goat cheese; mix until turns smooth. Scoop filling into a heavy, resealable 1-qt. plastic bag, compress to let air out, and secure the bag. Slice a small corner off the bag.

- Carefully insert the cut corner of the bag all the way to bottom of the open end of a blossom and pipe 1 tablespoon of filling inside. Collect petals and over the filling, drape them up, fully covering the filling. Put any extra petals over the top of the filled blossom to get them out of the way. Place filled squash blossoms inside the refrigerator for at least 30 minutes until cheese is firm and set.

- In a mixing bowl, combine cornstarch and self-rising flour; a little at a time, add in ice-cold water, until batter turns smooth and reaches thickness of pancake batter.

- Into a heavy skillet (like a cast iron pan), put vegetable oil to a depth of 1 inch and turn on the stove to medium heat. Warm oil until thermometer put in oil, without touching bottom, reads 350°F (175°C).Cautiously drop a single drop of batter into the oil and it should sizzle right away.

- Get squash blossoms from refrigerator and lightly sprinkle with all-purpose flour on all sides. Scrape off excess and then dip blossoms in batter. Allow the extra batter to drip off.

- Carefully lay coated squash blossoms in the oil on their sides; put in 6 at a time, cook until pale golden brown in color, 1 minute on the first side and 30 seconds to 1 minute on the other sides. Slightly cool prior to serving.

Nutrition Information

- Calories: 156 calories;

- Sodium: 214

- Total Carbohydrate: 13.3

- Cholesterol: 31

- Protein: 5

- Total Fat: 9.1

Fried Zucchini Squash Blossoms

Serving: 4

Ingredients

- 6 zucchini blossoms, or more to taste
- 1/3 cup soft goat cheese, at room temperature
- 1 egg yolk
- 1 scallion, diced
- 1/4 teaspoon freshly ground black pepper
- 1/4 teaspoon ground cayenne pepper
- 3/4 cup tapioca flour
- 1/2 cup arrowroot powder
- 1/2 cup coconut oil, melted, or as needed
- sea salt to taste

Direction

- Fill ice and cold water into a large bowl.

- Boil a big pot of lightly salted water. Add zucchini blossoms and cook for 20 seconds until slightly drooped. Drain in a colander and stop the cooking process by instantly immersing in ice water for some minutes. Line a plate with paper towels for draining.

- In a bowl, mix cayenne, pepper, scallion, egg yolk, and goat cheese until smooth.

- Spoon stuffing into a resealable plastic bag and secure, squash the air out as much as possible. Chop a small corner off the bag. Add 1 tablespoon of the stuffing to each zucchini blossom. Cover it by folding petals over the stuffing. Line on a plate.

- Chill filled zucchini blossoms for no less than 45 minutes, until cheese is condensed.

- In a shallow dish, stir arrowroot powder and tapioca flour.

- In a cast iron skillet, pour coconut oil to 1-inch depth. Heat until a thermometer pinned into the oil reaches 350°F (175°C).

- Lightly sprinkle cold zucchini blossoms over tapioca flour combination, shaking off the remainder. Fry in hot oil for about 1 minutes until golden. Turn over with tongs and fry for 1 minute more till golden on the second side. Transfer and drain zucchini blossoms onto a plate lined with paper towels. Flavor with sea salt.

Nutrition Information

- Calories: 465 calories;

- Cholesterol: 66

- Protein: 5.1

- Total Fat: 34.1

- Sodium: 181

- Total Carbohydrate: 37.2

Garlic Scape Goat Cheese Dip

Serving: 8

Ingredients

- 1 (8 ounce) package goat cheese, at room temperature

- 1 (4 ounce) package cream cheese, at room temperature

- 6 fresh garlic scapes, minced, or more to taste, divided

- 1/2 lemon, zested and juiced

- 1 teaspoon salt

- 1 clove garlic, minced

- 1/2 cup toasted pecans, chopped

Direction

- In a bowl, add garlic, salt, lemon juice, lemon zest, 5 garlic scapes, cream cheese, and goat cheese; use a fork to combine until mixed.
- Transfer the mixture into a serving bowl. Use toasted pecans and the remaining garlic scape to decorate.

Nutrition Information

- Calories: 219 calories;
- Cholesterol: 38
- Protein: 8.7
- Total Fat: 18.5
- Sodium: 481
- Total Carbohydrate: 6.6

Gefilte Fish

Serving: 8

Ingredients

- 1/2 teaspoon paprika
- 1/2 teaspoon ground black pepper
- 1/4 cup white sugar
- 5 eggs
- 1 1/2 tablespoons white sugar
- 4 teaspoons salt
- 4 teaspoons ground white pepper
- 3/4 cup matzo meal
- 3/4 cup ice water
- 2 onions
- 1 1/2 pounds salmon fillets
- 1 1/2 pounds red snapper fillets
- 1 pound black cod fillets
- 1 pound ling cod fillets
- 2 1/2 large onions

- 4 carrots
- 2 carrots

Direction

- Combine 2 1/2 onions, 4 carrots and fish together then grind them. Put the ground fish mixture into a wooden bowl. Mix in 1 egg at a time using a hand chopper. Put in 4 teaspoons of salt, white pepper and 1 1/2 tablespoons of sugar and keep chopping the mixture together using the hand chopper until everything is thoroughly combined. Mix in a few amount of ice water at a time during this entire process. Put in the matzo meal and chop the mixture altogether again. The consistency of the mixture should be thick enough to hold its shape when formed into an oval-shaped gefilte fish ball, and in case it is not, just add in additional matzo meal.

- While the fish mixture is being prepared, pour water into 2 big and heavy stock pots until it is halfway full. Slice 1 sliced carrot and 1 raw onion directly into each of the pots. You may put in the fish skins if you want. Season it with black pepper, paprika, 2 tablespoons of sugar and salt to taste. Let the mixture boil for 10 minutes over medium heat setting.

- Wet your hands and use it to form the prepared fish mixture into fish balls; drop the formed fish balls gently into the boiling stock mixture. Cover the pots a bit and let the fish balls cook for 2 hours over medium-low heat setting. Allow the fish balls to rest in the pot for 10 minutes first once it is done cooking before transferring the cooked fish balls gently into containers; pour the remaining stock mixture directly on top of the fish balls just to submerge them a bit. Keep it in the fridge before serving. You may store them in the fridge up to 6 days.

Nutrition Information

- Calories: 513 calories;
- Sodium: 1446
- Total Carbohydrate: 32.4

- Cholesterol: 248

- Protein: 62.1

- Total Fat: 14.2

Gorgonzola And Olive Stuffed Grape Leaves

Serving: 20

Ingredients

- 1 red bell pepper, chopped

- ground black pepper to taste

- 1 (8 ounce) jar grape leaves packed in brine

- 3 1/2 tablespoons chopped fresh garlic

- 2 tablespoons brown sugar

- salt to taste

- 3/4 cup chopped green olives

- 3/4 cup chopped kalamata olives

- 1/2 cup crumbled Gorgonzola cheese

- 3/4 cup chopped macadamia nuts

- 5 tablespoons chopped fresh basil leaves

- 4 roma (plum) tomatoes, seeded and chopped

Direction

- Combine brown sugar, garlic, bell pepper, tomatoes, basil, macadamia nuts, Gorgonzola cheese, kalamata olives and green olives in a bowl. Add pepper and salt for seasoning.

- Arrange each grape leaf flat, then generously place a heaped tablespoonful of the Gorgonzola and olive mixture in the middle. Roll or fold the leaves around the mixture. Chill before serving.

Nutrition Information

- Calories: 91 calories;

- Total Carbohydrate: 5.3

- Cholesterol: 4

- Protein: 2.2

- Total Fat: 7.3

- Sodium: 605

Greek Saganaki

Serving: 4

Ingredients

- 1/2 cup all-purpose flour
- 2 tablespoons olive oil
- freshly ground black pepper
- 2 large ripe tomatoes, sliced
- 8 ounces feta cheese
- 1 egg
- 1 teaspoon finely chopped fresh oregano
- 1 lemon, cut into wedges

Direction

- Slice feta into 2x3/8-in. square, around 8 slices. Beat oregano and egg in a small bowl. Dip each slice of the feta into the egg; shake off any excess; coat in flour.

- Place a frying pan on medium heat; heat olive oil. Cook cheese quickly, turning once, till golden. Using paper towels, pat dry.

- Spread the feta on a plate with thick tomato slices; season with black pepper; use lemon wedges to garnish.

Nutrition Information

- Calories: 302 calories;
- Protein: 12.1
- Total Fat: 20.4
- Sodium: 656
- Total Carbohydrate: 18.5
- Cholesterol: 97

Halibut Mango Ceviche

Serving: 6

Ingredients

- 1 mango - peeled, seeded and diced

- /4 cup chopped fresh parsley

- 1 teaspoon salt, or to taste

- 1 green bell pepper, seeded and finely chopped

- 1/2 cup finely chopped Vidalia or other sweet onion

- 1/2 cup finely chopped red onion

- 1 mango - peeled, seeded and diced

- 1/2 bunch chopped fresh cilantro

- 11 1/2 pounds skinless, boneless halibut, cut into 1/2 inch cubes

- 1/3 cup fresh lime juice

- 1/4 cup fresh lemon juice

- 1/4 cup tequila

- 3 jalapeno chile peppers, seeded and minced

Direction

- In a non-metallic bowl, mix 1 diced mango, minced jalapeno peppers, tequila, lemon juice, lime juice and cubed halibut. Refrigerate, covered, for 1 1/2 hours.

- Add red onion, sweet onion and green pepper when ceviche sat for 1 1/2 hours. Stir well. Refrigerate, covered, for 30 more minutes.

- Fold parsley, cilantro and leftover diced mango in. Before serving, season with salt to taste.

Nutrition Information

- Calories: 217 calories;
- Total Fat: 2.9
- Sodium: 456
- Total Carbohydrate: 18
- Cholesterol: 36
- Protein: 24.8

Exotic Ahi Tuna Nachos

Serving: 8

Ingredients

- 1 pound sushi-grade tuna, cut into 1/2-inch cubes
- 1 avocado, cubed
- 2 green onions, sliced
- 2 tablespoons soy sauce
- 1 medium lime
- Sauce:
- 2 tablespoons mayonnaise
- 2 teaspoons sriracha sauce
- 30 tortilla chips, crushed
- 2 teaspoons black sesame seeds (optional)

Direction

- In a bowl, mix soy sauce, green onion, avocado and tuna. On a hard surface, roll lime, then slice into wedges, and squeeze juice on top of tuna mixture.
- In a small resealable plastic bag, mix sriracha sauce and mayonnaise. Secure bag and rub sauce to mix.
- Split chips between 2 bowls. Put 1/2 of the tuna mixture into each bowl. Slice a small corner off the bag carrying the sauce and sprinkle over tuna.
- Sprinkle with sesame seeds to decorate.

Nutrition Information

- Calories: 164 calories;
- Total Fat: 8.7
- Sodium: 349
- Total Carbohydrate: 7.7
- Cholesterol: 27
- Protein: 14.8

Honey Black Pepper Chicken Wings

Serving: 8

Ingredients

- 2 teaspoons sesame seeds

- 4 cloves garlic, finely chopped

- 10 black peppercorns, coarsely ground

- 4 cups oil for deep frying

- 1 tablespoon sesame oil

- 2 tablespoons dark soy sauce

- 2 tablespoons white wine

- 1 1/2 tablespoons oyster sauce

- 1 tablespoon fresh lemon juice

- 3 tablespoons honey

- 1 pinch salt

- 1 slice fresh ginger root, finely chopped

- 8 chicken wings

- 2 red onions, minced

- 4 cloves garlic, finely chopped

- 1 slice fresh ginger root, minced

- water as needed

Direction

- In a nonporous glass bowl or dish, put the wings. In a blender, blend 1 slice ginger, 4 cloves garlic, and onions; pour in water as necessary to dilute. Rub the chicken pieces with this mixture.

- Mix salt, honey, lemon juice, oyster sauce, wine, soy sauce, sesame oil, and sesame seeds together in a small bowl. Stir thoroughly, and then mix in ground peppercorns, 4 cloves garlic, and 1 slice ginger. Add this mixture to the chicken and flip to coat. Put a cover on the dish and marinate in the fridge for about 30 minutes.

- In a deep fryer or a deep skillet, heat oil. In the hot oil, fry chicken until the juices run clear and fully cooked, about 10-15 minutes.

Nutrition Information

- Calories: 205 calories;

- Cholesterol: 10

- Protein: 3.5

- Total Fat: 15.8

- Sodium: 288

- Total Carbohydrate: 13.1

Honey Buttered Brie En Croute

Serving: 8

Ingredients

- 2 tablespoons honey, or more to taste

- 1 egg white, beaten

- 1 (8 ounce) round brie, sliced in half horizontally

- 1/4 cup slivered almonds

- 1 sheet frozen puff pastry, thawed

- 1/4 cup all-purpose flour

- 2 tablespoons butter, or more as needed

Direction

- Heat oven to 190°C (375°F) beforehand.

- Flour a pastry mat. Using a rolling pin, rolling the puff pastry out into a 1/4-inch sheet.

- On the puff pastry, lay half of the brie, rind side-down. Using a knife to cut the corners of the pastry off.

- Use a tablespoon of butter and 2 tablespoons of almonds to dab the top of brie. Use a tablespoon of honey to drizzle on. Use the other half of brie to cover, rind side-up. Place remaining honey, butter, and almonds on top.

- Wrapping around the wheel of brie with the puff pastry, pinching the seam together to seal them. Use egg white to brush. In a baking pan, lay brie en croute.

- In the preheated oven, allow to bake for 45-50 minutes till pastry gets golden brown.

Nutrition Information

- Calories: 344 calories;

- Total Carbohydrate: 21.9

- Cholesterol: 36

- Protein: 9.9

- Total Fat: 24.5

- Sodium: 281

How To Make Coquilles Saint Jacques

Serving: 4

Ingredients

- 4 large oven-safe scallop shells

- 1/4 cup shredded Gruyere cheese

- 1 pinch paprika

- 8 fresh tarragon leaves

- 1 pound sea scallops

- 1/2 cup heavy whipping cream

- 1 egg yolk

- 1 pinch cayenne pepper, or to taste

- 2 teaspoons minced fresh tarragon

- 2 tablespoons unsalted butter

- 1/2 cup diced shallots

- 1/2 pound white button mushrooms, sliced

- salt and freshly ground black pepper to taste

- 1 cup white wine

- 1 teaspoon lemon zest

Direction

- In big skillet, liquify butter on moderate heat; sauté shallots for 5 - 8 minutes in hot butter till clear. Mix in salt, black pepper and mushrooms. Switch heat to moderately-high; cook for 10 minutes, mixing frequently, till mushrooms turn golden brown in color.

- Add white wine on mixture of mushroom, dissolve any brown food bits on skillet's bottom into wine; let simmer. Put scallops in wine gently and poach in mixture of mushroom till just firm, approximately 2 minutes on every side. Turn the scallops into bowl. Strain mixture of mushroom in a separate bowl, separately reserve cooking liquid and mushrooms. Pour strained liquid back into skillet, add any gathered juices from scallops, and mix cream in. Boil and cook for 10 minutes, till cream sauce reduce by approximately 1/2. Mix frequently. Switch off the heat and cool mixture about a minute.

- Mix egg yolk to cream sauce quickly till incorporated. Turn skillet onto a work surface (like as a heat-safe countertop or chopping board) and mix 2 teaspoons of tarragon, lemon zest and cayenne pepper in sauce.

- Distribute mixture of mushroom among shells of scallop, scatter out mushrooms covering shells bottoms; on every portion, put approximately 3 scallops. Scoop cream sauce on top of scallops to cover; allow the sauce to drip down in mushrooms. Lightly scatter with cayenne or paprika and Gruyere cheese.

- Set broiler of oven to high. Crinkle a big aluminum foil sheet a bit and put on baking sheet. Arrange the filled shells on foil and lightly press to aid keep them level.

- Broil for 5 to 6 minutes approximately 10-inch away from heat till sauce bubbles and cheese turn light brown. Remove to napkins - lined - serving plates to keep shells from tipping; jazz every portion up using two crossed tarragon leaves.

Nutrition Information

- Calories: 374 calories;

- Protein: 26.3

- Total Fat: 21.6

- Sodium: 319

- Total Carbohydrate: 8.3

- Cholesterol: 162

Indonesian Pork Satay

Serving: 4

Ingredients

- 1/2 cup melted butter

- 1 1/2 pounds pork tenderloin, cut into 1 inch cubes

- skewers

- 1 cup roasted, salted Spanish peanuts

- 2 tablespoons lemon juice

- 2 tablespoons honey

- 1/2 cup soy sauce

- 2 teaspoons crushed coriander seed

- 2 cloves garlic

- 1/2 cup chopped green onions

- 1 tablespoon chopped fresh ginger root

- 1 teaspoon red pepper flakes

- 1/2 cup chicken broth

Direction

- Puree garlic, ginger, green onions, peanuts, coriander, honey, lemon juice, red pepper flakes, and soy sauce in a food processor until almost smooth. Add in butter and broth then process again.

- In a large, re-sealable bag, place pork cubes and pureed mixture; close and put in the refrigerator to marinate overnight or for at least 6 hours.

- Preheat grill on medium. Skewer pork cubes, reserving the marinade. Boil the marinade in a saucepan for 5 minutes; take some for basting and set the rest aside for dipping.

- Lightly grease the grille before cooking the kabobs for 10 to 15 minutes, turning and basting often with cooked marinade, until meat is browned. Serve dipping sauce on the side.

Nutrition Information

- Calories: 682 calories;

- Total Fat: 49.6

- Sodium: 2332

- Total Carbohydrate: 22.1

- Cholesterol: 156

- Protein: 41.6

Indonesian Satay

Serving: 6

Ingredients

- 1 pinch ground cumin 2 tablespoons white sugar

- 1 tablespoon lemon juice

- skewers

- 6 skinless, boneless chicken breast halves - cubed

- 1 tablespoon vegetable oil

- 1/4 cup minced onion

- 1 clove garlic, peeled and minced

- 1 cup water

- 1/2 cup chunky peanut butter

- 2 tablespoons soy sauce

- 3 tablespoons soy sauce

- 3 tablespoons tomato sauce

- 1 tablespoon peanut oil

- 2 cloves garlic, peeled and minced

- 1 pinch ground black pepper

Direction

- Mix tomato sauce, soy sauce, peanut oil, black pepper, garlic, and cumin in a bowl. Toss chicken in to coat. Cover the bowl and let sit in the fridge to marinate for at least 15 minutes, but not overnight as it will darken the meat too much.

- Preheat the grill on high.

- In a saucepan over medium heat, sauté garlic and onion in vegetable oil until slightly browned. Add in water, soy sauce, peanut butter, and sugar. Continue cooking with stirring until well-blended. Take saucepan away from the heat and stir in lemon juice. Set aside for use later.

- Lightly dab the grates with oil. Skewer the chicken, disposing of marinade. Grill for about 5 minutes per side, or until chicken is cooked through and its juices run clear. Serve the satays with the peanut sauce.

Nutrition Information

- Calories: 329 calories;

- Total Fat: 18.2

- Sodium: 957

- Total Carbohydrate: 11.8

- Cholesterol: 67

- Protein: 30.8

Italian Appetizer Bagna Cauda

Serving: 8

Ingredients

- 1 1/2 cups extra virgin olive oil
- 2 tablespoons heavy cream
- 4 tablespoons butter
- 4 cloves garlic, minced
- freshly ground black pepper to taste

Direction

- Mix butter and olive oil in a saucepan on medium heat; season using black pepper. Heat till butter melts; add garlic. Cook till garlic is soft yet not brown. Take off heat; mix in cream then serve warm.

Nutrition Information

- Calories: 444 calories;
- Total Fat: 49.1
- Sodium: 43
- Total Carbohydrate: 0.7
- Cholesterol: 20
- Protein: 0.2

Japanese Agedashi Deep Fried Tofu

Serving: 2

Ingredients

- 1 (12 ounce) package medium-firm silken tofu

- vegetable oil for deep frying, or as needed

- 3 tablespoons potato starch

- Sauce:

- 2 tablespoons water

- 2 teaspoons potato starch

- 2 tablespoons sake

- 1 tablespoon soy sauce

- 1 tablespoon mirin (Japanese sweet wine)

- 1 tablespoon fish stock, or to taste

- 1 teaspoon salt

- 1/4 carrot, cut into matchsticks

- 3 dried shiitake mushrooms, sliced into long, thin strips, or more to taste

- 1/2 Welsh onion (shironegi), cut into matchsticks

- 1 (1 inch) piece fresh ginger, grated, or to taste

Direction

- Slice tofu into squares. Put on a microwave-safe plate and cover using paper towel. Microwave for 3 to 4 minutes till moisture is vaporized.

- In a big saucepan, heat vegetable oil over medium-high heat. Generously coat tofu squares with potato starch. In hot oil, fry for 3 to 5 minutes each side till golden brown. Put in a bowl.

- In a bowl, combine 2 teaspoons potato starch and water to create the thickening agent.

- In a saucepan, mix fish stock, mirin, soy sauce and sake over medium-high heat. Boil; put mushrooms and carrots. Cook and mix for about 5 minutes till carrots are soft. Mix in thickening agent. Let cook and mix for about 2 minutes longer till flavors incorporate and sauce is thickened.

- Put sauce on top of tofu. Put ginger and Welsh onion on top.

Nutrition Information

- Calories: 268 calories;

- Cholesterol: 0

- Protein: 13.2

- Total Fat: 10.2

- Sodium: 1708

- Total Carbohydrate: 25.8

Mexican Ceviche

Serving: 12

Ingredients

- 1 tablespoon kosher salt

- ground black pepper to taste

- 1 cucumber, peeled and chopped

- 1 large tomato, coarsely chopped

- 1 jalapeno pepper, chopped

- 4 pounds shrimp

- 1 pound scallops

- 6 large limes, juiced

- 1 large lemon, juiced

- 1 small white onion, chopped

- 1 serrano pepper, chopped

- 1 bunch cilantro

- 1 tablespoon olive oil

Direction

- Toss the scallops and shrimp gently in a ceramic bowl or big glass with lemon juice and lime juice. Combine the pepper, salt, olive oil, cilantro, serrano, jalapeno, tomato, cucumber and onion. Cover the bowl and let the ceviche chill for an hour in the fridge, until the scallops and shrimp become opaque.

Nutrition Information

- Calories: 204 calories;
- Sodium: 859
- Total Carbohydrate: 10.6
- Cholesterol: 253
- Protein: 35.1
- Total Fat: 3

Kicked Up Olives

Serving: 18

Ingredients

- 4 cups mixed olives with pits

- 5 cloves garlic, peeled

- 1 tablespoon balsamic vinegar

- 1/4 teaspoon red pepper flakes

- 2 tangerines

- 3 slices sweet onion

- 4 sprigs fresh rosemary

- 2/3 cup extra-virgin olive oil

- 1 teaspoon fennel seeds, or to taste

Direction

- Preheat an oven to 120°C/250°F.

- Mix red pepper flakes, balsamic vinegar, garlic and olives in bowl.

- Peel tangerines carefully; cut peels to strips. Squeeze 1 tangerine's juice on olive mixture then add tangerine peel strips into olive mixture; toss well.

- Use a big aluminum foil piece to make a packet; put olive mixture in packet. Put rosemary and onion slices on olives; drizzle olive oil over. On top of mixture, sprinkle fennel seeds. Fold; seal packet. Put on baking sheet.

- In preheated oven, bake for 90 minutes till warmed; serve warm.

Nutrition Information

- Calories: 167 calories;

- Total Fat: 16.3

- Sodium: 490

- Total Carbohydrate: 4.8

- Cholesterol: 0

- Protein: 0.7

Kowloon's Chinese Chicken Wings

Serving: 11

Ingredients

- 3 pounds chicken wings
- 3 tablespoons salt
- 2 tablespoons white sugar
- 6 tablespoons water
- 6 tablespoons soy sauce
- 1 tablespoon gin
- 1/4 teaspoon ground ginger
- 1 quart vegetable oil for frying

Direction

- For the marinade, mix ginger, salt, water, sugar, soy sauce, and gin. Place the mixture into a resealable bag.

- Add the chicken into the bag and allow to marinade for 24 hours or as long as possible, and turn frequently.
- Set a large pan over medium-high heat.
- Fry the marinated chicken wings in hot oil for about 8 minutes each side or until golden brown.
- Serve.

Nutrition Information

Calories: 362 calories;

Cholesterol: 95

Protein: 23.2

Total Fat: 27.8

Sodium: 2485

Lavash Cracker Bread

Serving: 30

Ingredients

- 1 cup lukewarm water
- 1/4 cup whole wheat flour
- 1 (.25 ounce) envelope active dry yeast
- 1 teaspoon salt
- 3 cups all-purpose flour

Direction

- Mix yeast, whole wheat flour and water till moist in a big bowl; mix in 1 cup all-purpose flour and salt. Mix in leftover flour slowly using a wooden spoon/mixer with dough hook attachment.
- Knead for 8-10 minutes to create an elastic ball on a floured surface/in a mixer when dough comes together. If needed, add more water/flour to keep dough from getting too stiff/sticky. Put little oil

into bowl; turn dough to coat then cover. Rise for 1 hour till doubled in size in a warm place.

- Punch dough down; divide to 30 small walnut-sized pieces. To evenly divide, roll dough to a long log. Roll every piece to a ball; cover to rest using a damp kitchen towel for about 30 minutes.

- Preheat an oven to 260°C/500°F. Put baking sheet on middle oven rack to preheat at same time; don't grease.

- Roll every ball to 8-in. across circle; it should be paper thin, nearly translucent. It'll bubble up like a pita bread if too thick.

- Pull out oven shell; put as many crackers onto baking sheet as possible, 2-3. Close oven; bake for 3 minutes. Crackers should have small bubbles and lightly browned on top. For next bath, you might have to adjust thickness.

Nutrition Information

Calories: 50 calories;

Total Fat: 0.2

Sodium: 78

Total Carbohydrate: 10.4

Cholesterol: 0

Protein: 1.5

Lavosh

Serving: 10

Ingredients

- 2 1/2 cups all-purpose flour
- 1 teaspoon white sugar
- 1 teaspoon salt
- 2/3 cup water
- 1 egg white
- 2 tablespoons butter, melted
- 2 egg whites, beaten
- 2 tablespoons sesame seeds

Direction

- Prepare the oven by preheating to 400°F (200°C).
- Mix salt, sugar, and flour in a large bowl. Put in melted butter, 1 egg white, and water; combine well to form a stiff dough. Knead for about 5 minutes until the dough is smooth.

- Break the dough into 10 balls. Place each ball on a surface that is lightly floured and roll until paper-thin. Transfer to an ungreased baking sheet. Brush with egg white and dust with sesame seeds.
- Place in the preheated oven and bake for 10 to 12 minutes, until browned.

Nutrition Information

- Calories: 151 calories;
- Sodium: 266
- Total Carbohydrate: 24.8
- Cholesterol: 6
- Protein: 4.7
- Total Fat: 3.5

Lettuce Cups With Smoked Salmon And Eggs

Serving: 4

Ingredients

- 1 tablespoon extra-virgin olive oil

- 3/4 teaspoon sea salt

- 1/2 teaspoon freshly ground black pepper

- 4 hard-cooked eggs, chopped

- 6 slices smoked salmon

- 1 lemon, cut into wedges

- 1/4 cup chopped fresh parsley, or to taste

- 3 scallions, minced

- 2 tablespoons capers

- 2 tablespoons chopped red onion

- 6 leaves romaine lettuce

Direction

- In a bowl, combine red onion, capers, scallions and parsley, then put in pepper, salt and 1 tablespoon of olive oil; mix thoroughly. Beat in eggs.

- Place romaine leaves on a serving plate; arrange a slice of salmon onto each leaf and place on top with egg mixture. Use a lemon wedge and parsley to decorate each lettuce cup.

Nutrition Information

- Calories: 174 calories;

- Total Fat: 10.7

- Sodium: 855

- Total Carbohydrate: 5.9

- Cholesterol: 222

- Protein: 15

Liver Pate

Ingredients

- 1/4 cup chopped onion

- 3 tablespoons cooking sherry

- 3/4 cup butter, softened

- 1/4 teaspoon salt

- 3 cups water

- 1 pound chicken liver

- 1 onion, thinly sliced

- 1/4 teaspoon ground black pepper

- 1/8 teaspoon ground mace

Direction

- Place sliced onions, chicken livers, and water in a medium size saucepan. Make it boil, minimize the heat, then cover with a lid. Let it boil gently for about 20 minutes, or until cooked and liver becomes tender enough. Get the saucepan away from heat then strain and throw away the onions.

- Discard any hard portions of the liver too.

- Put the cooked livers in a food processor or in a blender, then mix well until it becomes smooth.

- Add in the mace, black pepper, salt, margarine or butter, sherry, and chopped onion; blend well. Slightly grease your hands, then turn pate mixture into a mound, then put it on a serving platter. Let it chill for 1 hour until serving time.

Nutrition Information

- Calories: 116 calories;

- Total Fat: 10

- Sodium: 135

- Total Carbohydrate: 1.3

- Cholesterol: 121

Lobster And Avocado Summer Roll With Mango Coulis

Serving: 6

Ingredients

For the Mango Coulis:

- 1/2 cup olive oil

- Kosher salt to taste

- 1 cup chopped ripe mango

- 2 tablespoons mirin

- 2 tablespoons fresh lime juice

For the Summer Rolls:

- 3 ounces mizuna or similar type peppery salad green

- 2 teaspoons chopped fresh mint

- 6 ounces ocean greens, sea vegetables

- 1 cup hearts of palm, cut into 1/4-inch sticks

- 12 (8 inch) Vietnamese spring roll wrappers (rice paper)

- 1 pound cooked lobster tails, sliced

- 1 (1/2 pound) avocado, sliced

- 2 ounces enoki mushrooms

- Kosher salt and fresh cracked pepper to taste

Direction

- Puree mango, lime juice, mirin and olive oil in a blender until smooth. Season sauce to taste with salt, and allow to stand in refrigerator until ready to serve.
- Soak a sheet of spring roll wrapper for 1/2 minute in a bowl of warm water, until it is just pliable. Shake gently to drain excess water.

- Place wrapper on work surface. Place a little sliced lobster, mizuna, avocado, mint, heart of palm, sea vegetables and mushrooms in a strip on bottom edge of the wrapper.
- Fold once towards the center.
- Fold in the sides over the filling and continue rolling into a neat cylinder.
- Repeat process until all ingredients are used up.
- Slice rolls diagonally and serve two per serving with mango sauce.

Nutrition Information

- Calories: 388 calories;
- Total Carbohydrate: 23.7
- Cholesterol: 54
- Protein: 19.4
- Total Fat: 24.6
- Sodium: 780

Mardi Gras Gator Meat Balls

Serving: 20

Ingredients

- 2 bunches fresh parsley

- 1 tablespoon black pepper

- 2 1/2 pounds cracker meal

- 1 medium head garlic

- 1/2 bunch celery

- 1 quart oil for frying

- 2 eggs

- 3 tablespoons dried savory

- 2 ounces salt

- 2 1/4 pounds potatoes, peeled and diced

- 5 1/4 pounds alligator meat

- 1 1/2 pounds onions
- 2 bunches green onions

Direction

- Boil a big pot of salted water. Add potatoes. Cook for 15 minutes until tender yet firm. Drain. Through a meat grinder, put potatoes, celery, parsley, green onions, onions and alligator meat into a big bowl. Mix in pepper, salt, savory and eggs until blended well. Shape to 1-oz golf ball sized balls. Roll in cracker meal.

- In a deep fryer, heat oil to 190 degrees C/375 degrees F. Fry meatballs until crisp and golden. On paper towels, drain.

Nutrition Information

- Calories: 586 calories;
- Total Fat: 11.1
- Sodium: 1129
- Total Carbohydrate: 56.4

- Cholesterol: 19

- Protein: 61.9

Brie Cheese Fondue

Serving: 4

Ingredients

- 2 cloves garlic, crushed
- 1 cup dry white wine
- 1/4 cup sherry
- 1 pound Brie cheese, rind removed and cubed
- 1 tablespoon cornstarch
- 1 pinch freshly grated nutmeg
- salt and white pepper to taste

Direction

- Rub the inside of the fondue pot with garlic and leave the crushed garlic pieces on the bottom of the pot. If you prefer, you can also use a regular cooking pan to cook the sauce then just move to the fondue pot. Pour the white wine and the sherry in the fondue pot and put it on medium-low heat.

- Coat the cheese cubes in cornstarch and once the wine is hot, add in the cheese. Start to stir slowly using a wooden spoon then mix together using a whisk. Stirring should be continuous so that the mixture would not scorch the bottom of the pot. Turn the heat off once the cheese has melted then add a bit of nutmeg by grating it in. Add salt and the pepper to season it. The sauce should be smooth in consistency and be able to coat a wooden spoon. If the sauce seems to be water, add in more of the cheese and if it's too thick, carefully add more wine.

- Set your fondue pot base up and keep the fondue warm, putting it on low heat. Set the table, take out the nice linen napkins and be proud of the meal you've prepared.

Nutrition Information

- Calories: 456 calories;

- Cholesterol: 114

- Protein: 23.7

- Total Fat: 31.5

- Sodium: 807

- Total Carbohydrate: 6.9

Meat And Potatoes Lumpia

Serving: 8

Ingredients

- 5 medium potatoes, peeled and cut into 1/2-inch chunks

- 1 pound lean ground beef

- 1/4 cup minced onion

- 1/4 cup minced green bell pepper

- salt to taste

- ground black pepper to taste

- 1 cup frozen mixed peas and carrots, thawed

- 1 cup canola oil

- 1 (16 ounce) package egg roll wrappers

Direction

- In a pot, place the potatoes then cover with a good amount of lightly salted water, and make it boil. And cook for 10 minutes, or until softened; strain.

- In a skillet set on medium heat, add the green bell pepper, onion, and beef. Add black pepper and salt to season. Cook until the onion is tender, and the beef is equally brown. Stir in carrots and peas and keep on cooking until heated well. Combine the potatoes with the beef mixture. In a big bowl. Keep in the refrigerator, covered, until fully cooled.

- In a deep fryer or big skillet, add oil and heat to 365°F (185°C).

- On a flat surface, lay the egg roll wrappers, and put 1/4 cup filling in the middle of each. Then fold to make egg rolls and enclose with dampened fingers. Fry the egg rolls in batches in the heated oil for approximately 3 minutes per side, until they are golden brown. Place on paper towels to drain on.

Nutrition Information

- Calories: 411 calories;

- Total Fat: 10.7

- Sodium: 374

- Total Carbohydrate: 59.1

- Cholesterol: 42

- Protein: 19

Moroccan Eggplant Dip

Serving: 12

Ingredients

- 1 1/2 pounds eggplant, unpeeled, cut into chunks
- 1 red bell pepper, seeded and cut into chunks
- 1/2 cup chopped fresh cilantro
- 1 teaspoon white sugar
- 1/4 teaspoon ground cayenne
- 2 tablespoons olive oil
- 1 (8 ounce) can tomato sauce
- 1/4 cup red wine vinegar
- 1 tablespoon ground cumin
- 1 teaspoon salt
- 2 cloves garlic, minced

Direction

- In a small bowl, mix together cayenne, sugar, salt, cumin, red wine vinegar and tomato sauce.

- In a large skillet, heat the olive oil over medium-low heat. Put in the garlic; cook while stirring for 2 mins until golden. Put in red bell pepper and eggplant; add to the tomato sauce mixture. Cover and simmer for 20 mins until red bell pepper and eggplant soften. Discard from the heat and allow to cool for 10 mins.

- Place eggplant mixture into the food processor, then pulse to the preferred consistency. Sprinkle dip with cilantro.

Nutrition Information

- Calories: 47 calories;

- Total Fat: 2.6

- Sodium: 295

- Total Carbohydrate: 6

- Cholesterol: 0

- Protein: 1.1

Moutabel

Serving: 64

Ingredients

- 4 medium eggplants
- 4 cloves garlic
- 1/4 cup fresh basil
- 2 fresh green chile peppers
- 1/4 cup tahini
- 4 tablespoons fresh lemon juice
- 1 teaspoon salt
- 1 sprig fresh mint
- 1 teaspoon olive oil

Direction

- Set oven to 200° C (400° F) and start preheating. Slightly oil a medium baking tray.

- Arrange eggplants on the baking tray. Put in the preheated oven and bake until seared and soft, about 30 minutes.

- Grind together green chile peppers, basil, and garlic in a food processor.

- Scoop eggplant from skins; put into the food processor to blend with garlic mixture.

- Pour the mixture into a medium serving dish. Mash in salt, lemon juice, and tahini using a fork. Put in olive oil and mint to garnish.

Nutrition Information

- Calories: 16 calories;
- Cholesterol: 0
- Protein: 0.6
- Total Fat: 0.6
- Sodium: 38
- Total Carbohydrate: 2.4

Mouth Watering Stuffed Mushrooms

Serving: 12

Ingredients

- 1/4 teaspoon onion powder

- 1/4 teaspoon ground cayenne pepper

- 1 tablespoon minced garlic

- 1 (8 ounce) package cream cheese, softened

- 1/4 cup grated Parmesan cheese

- 1/4 teaspoon ground black pepper

- 12 whole fresh mushrooms

- 1 tablespoon vegetable oil

Direction

- Set oven to 350°F (175°C) to preheat. Grease a baking sheet with cooking spray. Clean mushrooms using a damp paper towel. Gently break off mushroom stems. Chop stems very fine, removing any tough end of the stems.

- In a large skillet, heat oil over medium heat. Put chopped mushroom stems and garlic to pan and fry until moisture has evaporated, being careful not to burn the garlic. Put to one side and allow to cool.

- Once mushrooms and garlic are cool enough, mix in cayenne pepper, onion powder, black pepper, Parmesan cheese, and cream cheese until the mixture becomes very thick.

- Fill each mushroom cap with a liberal amount of stuffing mixture with a little spoon.

- Place the stuffed mushroom caps on the prepared baking sheet.

- Bake in the preheated oven until mushrooms are very hot and liquid begins to form under the caps, for 20 minutes.

Nutrition Information

- Calories: 88 calories;

- Sodium: 82

- Total Carbohydrate: 1.5

- Cholesterol: 22

- Protein: 2.7

THANK YOU

Thank you for choosing *Healthy Recipes For Beginners Appetizers* for improving your cooking skills! I hope you enjoyed making the recipes as much as tasting them! If you're interested in learning new recipes and new meals to cook, go and check out the other books of the series.

CPSIA information can be obtained
at www.ICGtesting.com
Printed in the USA
BVHW070858150321
602550BV00010B/1122